Discover the ...
ALTO SAXOPHONE

Chart Hits

Editorial, production and recording: Artemis Music Limited • Published 2003

International
MUSIC
Publications

Introduction

Welcome to DISCOVER THE LEAD, part of an instrumental series that provides beginners of all ages with fun, alternative material to increase their repertoire, but overall, enjoyment of their instrument!

For those of you just starting out, the idea of solo playing may sound rather daunting. DISCOVER THE LEAD will help you develop reading and playing skills, while increasing your confidence as a soloist.

You will find that the eight well-known songs have been carefully selected and arranged at an easy level - although interesting and musically satisfying. You will also notice that the arrangements can be used along with all the instruments in the series – flute, clarinet, alto saxophone, tenor saxophone, recorder, trumpet, violin and piano – making group playing possible!

The professionally recorded backing CD allows you to hear each song in two different ways:
- a complete demonstration performance with solo + backing
- backing only, so you can play along and DISCOVER THE LEAD!

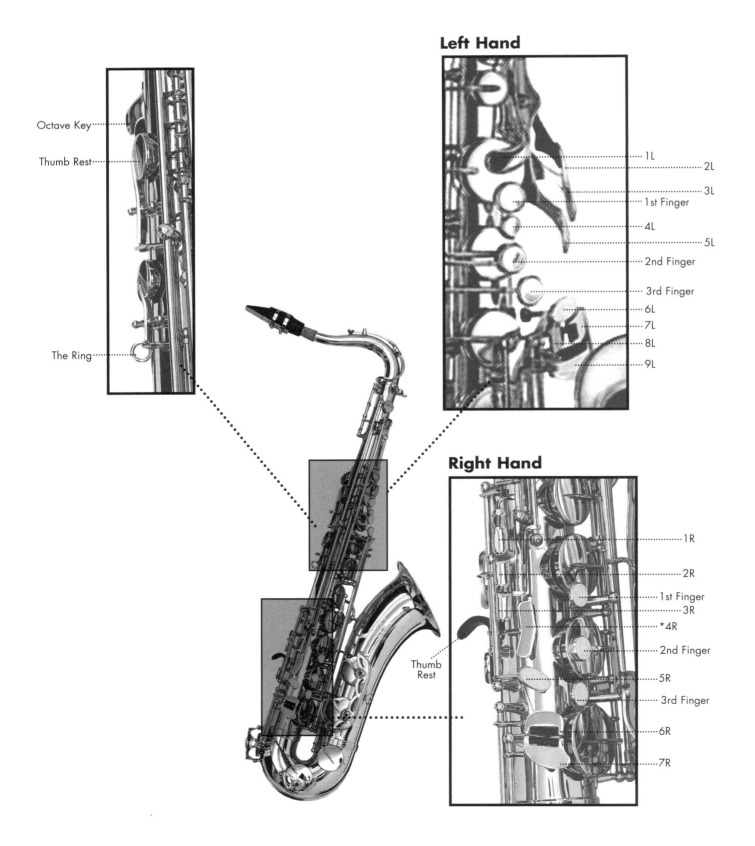

Wherever possible we have simplified the more
tricky rhythms and melodies, but if you are in any
doubt listen to the complete performance tracks and
follow the style of the players. Also, we have kept
marks of expression to a minimum, but feel free to
experiment with these – but above all, have fun!

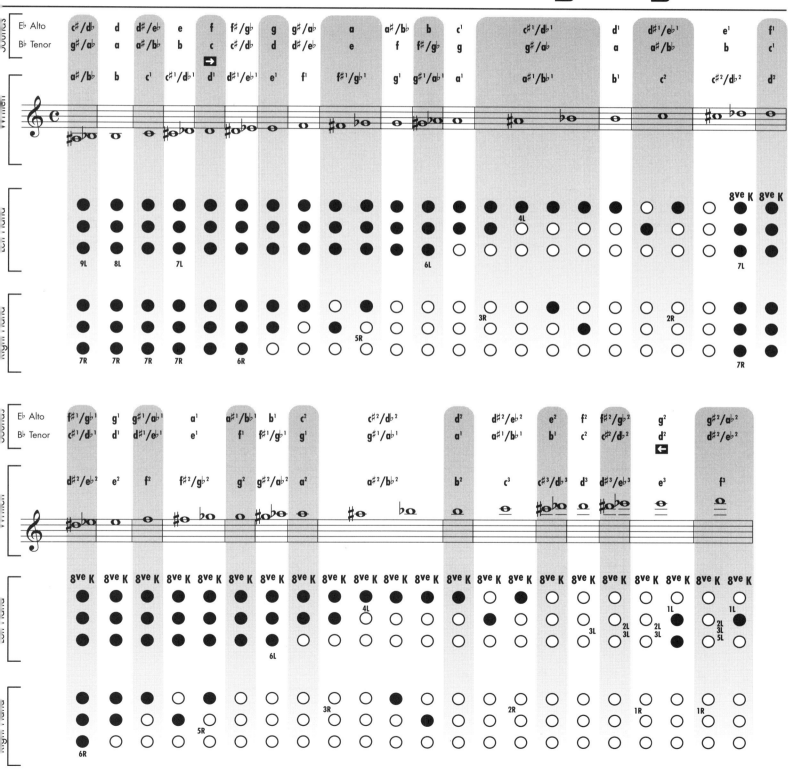

Indicates the lower limit of the best playing range

Indicates the upper limit of the best playing range

4

All The Things She Said

Demonstration

Backing

Words and Music by Trevor Horn,
Sergei Galoyan, Valerij Polienko,
Elener Kiper and Martin Kierszenbaum

Can't Nobody

Words and Music by Robert Reed,
Tony Fisher and Rich Harrison

Medium pop tempo

Feel

Demonstration   Backing

Words and Music by
Robert Williams and Guy Chambers

I'm With You

Words and Music by
Lauren Christy, David Alspach,
Graham Edwards and Avril Lavigne

Whatever your instrument is... you can now

TAKE THE LEAD *PLUS*

- Available in C, Bb, Eb and Bass Clef editions, this new concept opens up Take The Lead to a wider range of instruments, including cello, trombone, bassoon and baritone saxophone

- Flexible arrangements allowing players to team up with any number of instruments able to read from one of the 4 editions – C, Bb, Eb and Bass Clef.

- Each edition contains the full instrumental score in either 2,3 or 4 parts

- Professionally recorded backing tracks that re-create the sound of the original recordings.

TAKE THE LEAD

- Each book comes with a professionally recorded CD containing full backing tracks for you to play along with, and demonstration tracks to help you learn the songs

- Ideal for solo or ensemble use - in each edition, songs are in the same concert pitch key

- Each book includes carefully selected and edited top line arrangements; chord symbols in concert pitch for use by piano or guitar

- Suitable for intermediate players
  "A great way to get some relaxing playing done in between the serious stuff" **Sheet Music Magazine**

Discover The Lead

- This new 'spin off' of the Take The Lead series is ideal for beginners of all ages, grades 1-3

- The books contain simplified arrangements of well-known tunes to help the beginner develop reading and playing skills, while increasing confidence as a soloist

- Includes a useful fingering chart plus a CD with full backing and demonstration tracks

- Lots of helpful hints and technical tips to help you get to know your instrument

SHARE THE LEAD

- All pieces have been carefully selected and arranged at an easy level to provide fun material for today's instrumentalists

- All the arrangements work not only as duets for one particular instrument, but with all other instruments in the series (i.e. the flute book works with the clarinet book)

- The professionally recorded CD allows you to hear each song in 4 different ways – a complete demonstration of the track; part two plus backing so you can play along on part one; part one plus backing so you can play along on part two; and the backing only so you and a friend can Share The Lead!

A

Air That I Breathe, The TTL - 90s Hits
Air On A G String (Bach) DTL - Classical Collection
All Through The Night TTL - British Isles Folk Songs
Amazed TTL - Ballads
Angels TTL - 90s Hits
Animaniacs Theme DTL – Kids' Film & TV Themes
Anything Is Possible DTL – Smash Hits
Ave Maria (Schubert) DTL - Classical Collection
Away In A Manger DTL - Christmas Carols

B

Bailamos TTL - Latin
Be-Bop-A-Lula TTL - Rock 'n' Roll
Beautiful Stranger STL - Film & TV Hits
Beauty School Dropout TTL - Grease
Because You Loved Me - Movie Hits
Believe TTL - Number One Hits
Birdland TTL - Jazz
Blue Monday TTL - Movie Hits
Blue Suede Shoes TTL - Rock 'n' Roll
Blueberry Hill TTL - Rock 'n' Roll
Bop Bop Baby DTL – Smash Hits

C

Can We Fix It? DTL – Kids' Film & TV Themes
Can't Fight The Moonlight TTL Plus – Pop Hits
Can't Get You Out Of My Head TTL Plus – Pop Hits
Careless Whisper TTL - Number One Hits
Charlie's Angels STL - Film & TV Hits
Chattanooga Choo Choo TTL - Swing
Cherry Pink And Apple Blossom White TTL – Latin
Chitty Chitty Bang Bang DTL – Kids' Film & TV Themes
Choo Choo Ch'Boogie TTL - Swing
C'mon Everybody TTL - Rock 'n' Roll
Coronation Street TTL - TV Themes
Christmas Song, The (Chestnuts Roasting On An Open Fire) TTL - Christmas Songs

D

Dance Of The Sugar Plum... The Nutcracker (Tchaikovsky) TTL - Classical Collection
Dancing Queen TTL - Number One Hits STL - Chart Hits
Desafinado TTL - Jazz
Do Nothin' 'Till You Hear From Me - TTL Plus Jazz Standards
Don't Get Around Much Anymore TTL - Jazz
Don't Say You Love Me STL - Film & TV Hits
Don't Tell Me DTL - Pop Hits

E

Eternity TTL Plus – Pop Hits
Everybody Needs Somebody To Love TTL - The Blues Brothers
(Everything I Do) I Do It For You TTL - Movie Hits

F

Fallin' TTL Plus – Pop Hits
Fascinating Rhythm TTL - Jazz
Fame TTL – Musicals
First Nowell, The DTL - Christmas Carols
Flying Without Wings TTL - Number One Hits STL - Chart Hits
Food Glorious Food TTL - Musicals
Frosty The Snowman TTL - Christmas Songs
Frozen TTL - 90s Hits

G

Genie In A Bottle DTL - Pop Hits
Get Here TTL - Ballads
Gimme Some Lovin' TTL - The Blues Brothers
Greased Lightnin' TTL - Grease
Great Balls Of Fire TTL - Rock 'n' Roll
Green Door, The TTL - Rock 'n' Roll
Greensleeves TTL - British Isles Folk Songs
Guantanamera TTL - Latin

H

Hall Of The Mountain King from Peer Gynt (Grieg) TTL - Classical Collection
Handbags & Gladrags TTL Plus - Pop Hits
Hark! The Herald Angels Sing DTL – Christmas Carols
Have Yourself A Merry Little Christmas TTL - Christmas Songs
Hedwig's Theme DTL – Kids' Film & TV Themes
Hero DTL - Smash Hits
Hey Baby TTL - Smash Hits
Holler DTL - Pop Hits
How Do I Live TTL - 90s Hits STL - Chart Hits
How You Remind Me DTL - Smash Hits

I

I Believe STL - Film & TV Hits
I Don't Want To Miss A Thing TTL - 90s Hits TTL - Movie Hits TTL - Ballads
I Want Love TTL Plus – Pop Hits
I Will Always Love You TTL - Movie Hits TTL - Number One Hits
I'll Be There For You (Theme from Friends) TTL - 90s Hits TTL - TV Themes STL - Film & TV Hits
I've Got A Gal In Kalamazoo TTL - Swing
If I Were A Rich Man TTL - Musicals
I'm Like A Bird TTL – Smash Hits
In The Mood TTL - Swing
It Don't Mean A Thing (If It Ain't Got That Swing) TTL - Swing, TTL PLus Jazz Standards
It's OK DTL - Smash Hits
It's Raining Men TTL – Smash Hits TTL Plus – Pop Hits
It's Raining On Prom Night TTL - Grease

J

Jailhouse Rock TTL - Rock 'n' Roll
Jeepers Creepers - TTL Plus Jazz Standards
Jersey Bounce TTL - Swing
Just A Little DTL - Smash Hits

L

La Bamba TTL - Latin
La Donna E Mobile From Rigoletto (Verdi) DTL - Classical Collection
La Isla Bonita TTL - Latin
Lady Marmalade TTL – Smash Hits
Largo From New World Symphony (Dvorak) DTL - Classical Collection
Leaving Of Liverpool, The TTL - British Isles Folk Songs
Let's Twist Again TTL - Rock 'n' Roll

Life Is A Rollercoaster DTL - Pop Hits
Little Bit More, A TTL - Ballads
Little Donkey TTL - Christmas Songs
Livin' La Vida Loca TTL - Number One Hits TTL - Latin
Loch Lomond TTL - British Isles Folk Songs
Look At Me, I'm Sandra Dee TTL - Grease
Love's Got A Hold On My Heart STL - Chart Hits
Lullaby From Wiegenlied (Brahms) DTL - Classical Collection

M

Match Of The Day TTL - TV Themes
(Meet) The Flintstones TTL - TV Themes
Men Behaving Badly TTL - TV Themes
Men Of Harlech TTL - British Isles Folk Songs
Millennium DTL - Pop Hits
Minnie The Moocher TTL - The Blues Brothers
Misty TTL - Jazz, TTL Plus Jazz Standards
Moonlight In Vermont - TTL PLus Jazz Standards
More Than Words STL - Chart Hits
Morning From Peer Gynt (Greig) DTL - Classical Collection
My Funny Valentine TTL - Jazz
My Heart Will Go On TTL - 90s Hits TTL – Ballads STL - Chart Hits

N

Number One DTL - Kids' Film & TV Themes

O

O Come All Ye Faithful DTL – Christmas Carols
O Little Town Of Bethlehem DTL – Christmas Carols
Ode To Joy From Symphony No. 9 (Beethoven) DTL - Classical Collection
Old Landmark, The TTL - The Blues Brothers
On Green Dolphin Street - TTL Plus Jazz Standards
Once In Royal David's City DTL - Christmas Carols
One O'Clock Jump TTL - Jazz
One Step Closer DTL - Smash Hits
Out Of Reach TTL – Smash Hits
Oye Mi Canto (Hear My Voice) TTL - Latin
Over The Rainbow TTL – Musicals DTL – Kids' Film & TV Themes

P

Peak Practice TTL - TV Themes
Pennsylvania 6-5000 TTL - Swing
Pokemon Main Theme DTL Kids' Film & TV Themes
Polovtsian Dances from Prince Igor (Borodin) TTL - Classical Collection
Pure Shores STL - Film & TV Hits

R

Radetzky March (Strauss) TTL - Classical Collection
Reach DTL - Pop Hits
Rose, The TTL - Ballads
Rudolph The Red-Nosed Reindeer TTL - Christmas Songs

S

Santa Claus Is Comin' To Town TTL - Christmas Songs
Say What You Want DTL - Pop Hits
Scarborough Fair TTL - British Isles Folk Songs
Scooby Doo Theme DTL Kids' Film & TV Themes
Searchin' My Soul STL - Film & TV Hits
Seasons In The Sun DTL - Pop Hits
Send In The Clowns TTL - Musicals
The Shadow Of Your Smile - TTL PLus Jazz Standards
Shake A Tail Feather TTL - The Blues Brothers
She Caught The Katy And Left Me A Mule To Ride TTL - The Blues Brothers
Sheep May Safely Graze (Bach) TTL - Classical Collection
Silent Night DTL - Christmas Carols
Simpsons, The TTL - TV Themes
Singin' In The Rain TTL - Musicals
Skye Boat Song, The TTL - British Isles Folk Songs
Sleigh Ride TTL - Christmas Songs
Something About The Way You Look Tonight TTL - 90s Hits
Soul Limbo TTL - Latin
Spring From The Four Seasons (Vivaldi) DTL - Classical Collection
Stardust - TTL Plus Jazz Standards
Star Wars (Main Theme) TTL - Movie Hits
String Of Pearls, A TTL - Swing
Summer Nights TTL - Grease
Summertime TTL - Jazz
Swan, The from Carnival of the Animals (Saint-Säens) TTL - Classical Collection
Swear It Again TTL - Ballads
Sweet Home Chicago TTL - The Blues Brothers
Symphony No. 40 in G Minor, 1st Movement (Mozart) TTL - Classical Collection

T

The Way To Your Love TTL - Smash Hits
There Are Worse Things I Could Do TTL - Grease
There You'll Be TTL - Smash Hits
Think TTL - The Blues Brothers
Tomorrow TTL - Musicals
Toreador's Song, The from Carmen (Bizet) TTL - Classical Collection

U

Uptown Girl TTL – Smash Hits

W

We Go Together TTL - Grease
We Three Kings Of Orient Are DTL - Christmas Carols
What If TTL Plus - Pop Hits
When Irish Eyes Are Smiling TTL - British Isles Folk Songs
When You Say Nothing At All TTL - Number One Hits STL - Chart Hits STL - Film & TV Hits
Whole Again TTL – Smash Hits
Wind Beneath My Wings, The TTL - Movie Hits TTL - Ballads
Winter Wonderland TTL - Christmas Songs
Wouldn't It Be Lovely TTL - Musicals

X

X-Files, The TTL - TV Themes

Y

You Needed Me TTL - Number One Hits
STL - Chart Hits
You Can Leave Your Hat On TTL - Movie Hits
You're The One That I Want TTL - Grease

Take The Lead

90s Hits
Air That I Breathe - I'll Be There For You - Something About The Way You Look Tonight - Frozen - How Do I Live - Angels - My Heart Will Go On - I Don't Want To Miss A Thing

Movie Hits
Because You Loved Me, Blue Monday, (Everything I Do) I Do It For You, I Don't Want To Miss A Thing, I Will Always Love You, Star Wars, The Wind Beneath My Wings

TV Themes
Coronation Street, I'll Be There For You (Theme from Friends), Match Of The Day, (Meet) The Flintstones, Men Behaving Badly, Peak Practice, The Simpsons, The X-Files

The Blues Brothers
She Caught The Katy And Left Me A Mule To Ride - Gimme Some Lovin' - Shake A Tail Feather - Everybody Needs Somebody To Love - The Old Landmark - Think - Minnie The Moocher - Sweet Home Chicago

Christmas Songs
Winter Wonderland - Little Donkey - Frosty The Snowman - Rudolph The Red Nosed Reindeer - Christmas Song (Chestnuts Roasting On An Open Fire) - Have Yourself A Merry Little Christmas - Santa Claus Is Comin' To Town - Sleigh Ride

Swing
Chattanooga Choo Choo - Choo Choo Ch'Boogie - I've Got A Gal In Kalamazoo - In The Mood - It Don't Mean A Thing (If It Ain't Got That Swing) - Jersey Bounce - Pennsylvania 6-5000 - A String Of Pearls

Jazz
Birdland - Desafinado - Don't Get Around Much Anymore - Fascinating Rhythm - Misty - My Funny Valentine - One O'Clock Jump - Summertime

Latin
Bailamos - Cherry Pink And Apple Blossom White - Desafinado - Guantanamera - La Bamba - La Isla Bonita - Oye Mi Canto (Hear My Voice) - Soul Limbo

Number One Hits
Believe, Cher - Careless Whisper, George Michael - Dancing Queen, Abba - Flying Without Wings, Westlife - I Will Always Love You, Whitney Houston - Livin' La Vida Loca, Ricky Martin - When You Say Nothing At All, Ronan Keating - You Needed Me, Boyzone

Classical Collection
Sheep May Safely Graze (Bach) - Symphony No. 40 in G Minor, 1st Movement (Mozart) - The Toreador's Song from Carmen (Bizet) - Hall Of The Mountain King from Peer Gynt (Grieg) - Radetzky March (Strauss) - Dance Of The Sugar Plum Fairy from The Nutcracker (Tchaikovsky) - Polovtsian Dances from Prince Igor (Borodin) - The Swan from Carnival of the Animals (Saint-Saëns)

Rock 'n' Roll
Be-Bop-A-Lula - Blue Suede Shoes - Blueberry Hill - C'mon Everybody - Great Balls Of Fire - The Green Door - Jailhouse Rock - Let's Twist Again

Ballads
Amazed - Get Here - I Don't Want To Miss A Thing - A Little Bit More - My Heart Will Go On - The Rose - Swear It Again - The Wind Beneath My Wings

British Isles Folk Songs
All Through The Night - Greensleeves - The Leaving Of Liverpool - Loch Lomond - Men Of Harlech - Scarborough Fair - The Skye Boat Song - When Irish Eyes Are Smiling

Musicals
Fame – Food Glorious Food – If I Were A Rich Man – Over The Rainbow – Send In The Clowns – Singin' In The Rain – Tomorrow – Wouldn't It Be Lovely

Smash Hits
I'm Like A bird – It's Raining Men – Lady Marmalade – Out Of Reach – There You'll Be – Uptown Girl – The Way to Your Love – Whole Again

Grease
Beauty School Dropout – Greased Lightnin' – It's Raining On Prom Night – Look At Me, I'm Sandra Dee – Summer Nights – There Are Worse Things I Could Do – We Go Together – You're The One That I Want

Take The The Lead Plus

Pop Hits
Can't Fight The Moonlight – Bop Bop Baby – Hero – Hey Baby – How You Remind Me – It's OK – Just A Little – One Step Closer

Jazz Standards
Do Nothin' 'Till You Hear From Me - It Don't Mean A Thing (If It Ain't Got That Swing) - Jeepers Creepers - Misty - Moonlight In Vermont - On Green Dolphin Street - Stardust - The Shadow Of Your Smile

Share The The Lead

Chart Hits
Dancing Queen - Flying Without Wings - How Do I Live - Love's Got A Hold On My Heart - My Heart Will Go On - More Than Words - When You Say Nothing At All - You Needed Me

Film & TV Hits
Beautiful Stranger - Charlie's Angels - Don't Say You Love Me - I Believe - I'll Be There For You - Pure Shores - Searchin' My Soul - When You Say Nothing At All

Discover The Lead

Pop Hits
Don't Tell Me - Genie In A Bottle - Holler - Life Is A Rollercoaster - Millennium - Reach - Say What You Want - Seasons In The Sun

Classical Collection
Air On A G String (Bach) - Ave Maria (Schubert) - La Donna E Mobile from Rigoletto (Verdi) - Largo from New World Symphony (Dvorak) - Lullaby from Wiegenlied (Brahms) - Morning from Peer Gynt (Greig) - Ode To Joy from Symphony No. 9 (Beethoven) - Spring from The Four Seasons (Vivaldi)

Christmas Carols
Away In A Manger – The First Nowell – Hark! The Herald Angels Sing – O Come All Ye Faithful – O Little Town Of Bethlehem – Once In Royal David's City – Silent Night – We Three Kings Of Orient Are

Kids' Film & TV Themes
Animaniacs Theme – Can We Fix It? – Chitty Chitty Bang Bang – Hedwig's Theme – Number One – Over The Rainbow – Pokemon Main Theme – Scooby Doo Theme

Smash Hits
Anything Is Possible – Bop Bop Baby – Hero – Hey Baby – How You Remind Me – It's OK – Just A Little – One Step Closer

Whatever your instrument is...
you can now
TAKE, DISCOVER & SHARE

Available for Violin
7240A TTL Swing
7177A TTL Jazz
7084A TTL The Blues Brothers
7025A TTL Christmas Songs
7006A TTL TV Themes
6912A TTL Movie Hits
6728A TTL 90s Hits
7263A TTL Latin
7313A TTL Number One Hits
7508A TTL Classical Collection
7715A TTL Rock 'n' Roll
8487A TTL Ballads
9068A TTL British Isles Folk Songs
9245A TTL Musicals
9406A TTL Smash Hits
9656A TTL Grease
7287A STL Chart Hits
8493A STL Film & TV Hits
8856A DTL Pop
9165A DTL Classical Collection
9306A DTL Christmas Carols
9566A DTL Kids' Film & TV Themes
9731A DTL Smash Hits

Available for Clarinet
7173A TTL Jazz
7236A TTL Swing
7080A TTL The Blues Brothers
7023A TTL Christmas Songs
7004A TTL TV Themes
6909A TTL Movie Hits
6726A TTL 90s Hits
7260A TTL Latin
7309A TTL Number One Hits
7505A TTL Classical Collection
7711A TTL Rock 'n' Roll
8483A TTL Ballads
9064A TTL British Isles Folk Songs
9241A TTL Musicals
9402A TTL Smash Hits
9652A TTL Grease
7285A STL Chart Hits
8491A STL Film & TV Hits
8852A DTL Pop
9161A DTL Classical Collection
9302A DTL Christmas Carols
9562A DTL Kids' Film & TV Themes
9727A DTL Smash Hits

Available for Drums
7179A TTL Jazz
7027A TTL Christmas Songs

Available for Trumpet
7083A TTL The Blues Brothers
7239A TTL Swing
7176A TTL Jazz
7262A TTL Latin
7312A TTL Number One Hits
7503A TTL Christmas Songs
7507A TTL Classical Collection
7714A TTL Rock 'n' Roll
8486A TTL Ballads
9067A TTL British Isles Folk Songs
9244A TTL Musicals
9405A TTL Smash Hits
9655A TTL Grease
8494A STL Film & TV Hits
8855A DTL Pop
9164A DTL Classical Collection
9305A DTL Christmas Carols
9565A DTL Kids' Film & TV Themes
9730A DTL Smash Hits

Available for Tenor Saxophone
6911A TTL Movie Hits
7238A TTL Swing
7175A TTL Jazz
7082A TTL The Blues Brothers
7311A TTL Number One Hits
7637A TTL Christmas Songs
7713A TTL Rock 'n' Roll
8485A TTL Ballads
9066A TTL British Isles Folk Songs
9243A TTL Musicals
9404A TTL Smash Hits
9654A TTL Grease
9163A DTL Classical Collection
8854A DTL Pop
9304A DTL Christmas Carols
9564A DTL Kids' Film & TV Themes
9729A DTL Smash Hits

Available for Piano
7178A TTL Jazz
7026A TTL Christmas Songs
7364A TTL Latin
7441A TTL Number One Hits
7509A TTL Classical Collection
7716A TTL Rock 'n' Roll
8488A TTL Ballads
9069A TTL British Isles Folk Songs
9246A TTL Musicals
9407A TTL Smash Hits
9657A TTL Grease
8857A DTL Pop
9166A DTL Classical Collection
9307A DTL Christmas Carols
9567A DTL Kids' Film & TV Themes
9732A DTL Smash Hits

Available for Flute
6725A TTL 90s Hits
7079A TTL The Blues Brothers
7235A TTL Swing
7172A TTL Jazz
7022A TTL Christmas Songs
7003A TTL TV Themes
6908A TTL Movie Hits
7259A TTL Latin
7310A TTL Number One Hits
7504A TTL Classical Collection
7710A TTL Rock 'n' Roll
8482A TTL Ballads
9063A TTL British Isles Folk Songs
9240A TTL Musicals
9401A TTL Smash Hits
9651A TTL Grease
7284A STL Chart Hits
8490A STL Film & TV Hits
8851A DTL Pop
9160A DTL Classical Collection
9301A DTL Christmas Carols
9561A DTL Kids' Film & TV Themes
9726A DTL Smash Hits

Available for Alto Saxophone
7005A TTL TV Themes
7237A TTL Swing
7174A TTL Jazz
7081A TTL The Blues Brothers
7024A TTL Christmas Songs
6910A TTL Movie Hits
6727A TTL 90s Hits
7261A TTL Latin
7308A TTL Number One Hits
7506A TTL Classical Collection
7712A TTL Rock 'n' Roll
8484A TTL Ballads
9065A TTL British Isles Folk Songs
9242A TTL Musicals
9403A TTL Smash Hits
9653A TTL Grease
7286A STL Chart Hits
8492A STL Film & TV Hits
8853A DTL Pop
9162A DTL Classical Collection
9303A DTL Christmas Carols
9563A DTL Kids' Film & TV Themes
9728A DTL Smash Hits

Available for C Instruments
9685A TTL Plus Pop Hits
9771A TTL Plus Jazz Standards

Available for Bb Instruments
9686A TTL Plus Pop Hits
9772A TTL Plus Jazz Standards (Brass)
9773A TTL Plus Jazz Standards (Woodwind)

Available for Eb Instruments
9687A TTL Plus Pop Hits
9774A TTL Plus Jazz Standards (Brass)
9775A TTL Plus Jazz Standards (Woodwind)

Available for Bass Clef Instruments
9692A TTL Plus Pop Hits
9792A TTL Plus Jazz Standards

Teachers' Pack
9793A TTL Plus Jazz Standards

Available from:

TTL05

Published by:

IMP
International MUSIC Publications

International Music Publications Ltd
Griffin House
161 Hammersmith Road
London
England W6 8BS

Registered In England No. 2703274
Warner Music Group An AOL Time Warner Company

No Good Advice

Demonstration   Backing

Words and Music by Miranda Cooper,
Brian Higgins, Timothy Powell,
Matthew Gray, Lisa Cowling, Nick Coler,
Shawn Mahan, Tim Larcombe and Lene Nystrom

Rock Your Body

Demonstration

Backing

Words and Music by Chad Hugo,
Pharrell Williams and Justin Timberlake

Moderate dance groove

Say Goodbye

Demonstration   Backing

Words and Music by
Christopher Braide and Cathy Dennis

Sorry Seems To Be
The Hardest Word

Demonstration

Backing

Words by Bernie Taupin
Music by Elton John

Medium pop ballad

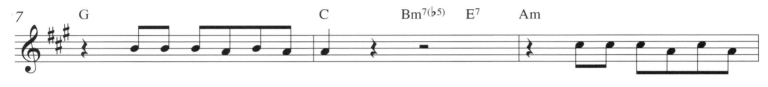

Care Of Your Saxophone

Things You Should Have

Cork grease or Vaseline
Medium bristle artist's paint brush
Weighted cloth swab for inside
Two cloths, one for the outside and one for the mouthpiece
Key oil
At least one extra reed

Putting Your Saxophone Together

When putting your Saxophone together (or taking it apart) you must be gentle with the keys and rods as they can be very easily damaged. Use a small amount of cork grease or Vaseline if necessary.

Once you have assembled the mouthpiece you should use a twisting motion to insert it into the crook, then loosen the tension screw on the main body and fit the crook and mouthpiece.

Then check that the mouthpiece is in line with the thumb rest and that the reed feels comfortable.

Then tighten the tension screw and attach your neck strap, making sure that it is adjusted for you to play.

Storing Your Saxophone

When putting your Saxophone into the case, make sure that you have loosened the mouthpiece ligature to stop it warping. Also don't forget to take the reed out and wash and dry it properly, then place it in the reed holder.

Keeping Your Saxophone Clean

Use a soft cloth to keep your Saxophone free of fingerprints and don't forget that your hands will perspire while you are playing.

You can use your swab to clean the inside of your Saxophone. You should do this after playing and use your crook swab to clean inside thoroughly. Carefully clean the mouthpiece and reed with warm soapy water and then rinse.

You can use your paintbrush after playing to clean the keys and rods properly.

The screws and springs can develop rust; so the occasional drop of oil will help prevent this (don't get any on the pads).

A Guide to Notation

Note and Rest Values

This chart shows the most commonly used note values and rests.

Name of note (UK)	Semibreve	Minim	Crotchet	Quaver	Semiquaver
Name of note (USA)	Whole note	Half note	Quarter note	Eighth note	Sixteenth note
Note symbol	𝅝	𝅗𝅥	𝅘𝅥	𝅘𝅥𝅮	𝅘𝅥𝅯
Rest symbol	▬	▬	𝄽	𝄾	𝄿
Value per beats	4	2	1	1/2	1/4

Repeat Bars

When you come to a double dotted bar, you should repeat the music between the beginning of the piece and the repeat mark.

When you come to a repeat bar you should play again the music that is between the two dotted bars.

First, second and third endings

The first time through you should play the first ending until you see the repeat bar. Play the music again and skip the first time ending to play the second time ending, and so on.

D.C. (Da Capo)

When you come to this sign you should return to the beginning of the piece.

D.C. al Fine

When this sign appears, go back to the beginning and play through to the *Fine* ending marked. When playing a *D.C. al Fine*, you should ignore all repeat bars and first time endings.

D.S. (Dal Segno)

Go back to the 𝄋 sign.

D.S. al Fine

Go to the sign 𝄋 and play the ending labelled *(Fine)*.

D.S. al Coda

Repeat the music from the 𝄋 sign until the ⊕ or *To Coda* signs, and then go to the coda sign. Again, when playing through a *D. 𝄋 al Coda*, ignore all repeats and don't play the first time ending.

Accidentals

Flat ♭ - When a note has a flat sign before it, it should be played a semi tone lower.

Sharp ♯ - When a note has a sharp sign before it, it should be played a semi tone higher.

Natural ♮ - When a note has a natural sign before it, it usually indicates that a previous flat or sharp has been cancelled and that it should be played at its actual pitch.

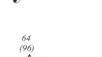

Bar Numbers

Bar numbers are used as a method of identification, usually as a point of reference in rehearsal. A bar may have more than one number if it is repeated within a piece.

Pause Sign

A pause is most commonly used to indicate that a note/chord should be extended in length at the player's discretion. It may also indicate a period of silence or the end of a piece.

Dynamic Markings

Dynamic markings show the volume at which certain notes or passages of music should be played. For example

pp	= very quiet	*mf*	= moderately loud
p	= quiet	*f*	= loud
mp	= moderately quiet	*ff*	= very loud

Time Signatures

Time signatures indicate the value of the notes and the number of beats in each bar. The top number shows the number of beats in the bar and the bottom number shows the value of the note.